WYNDS OF PASSION: THE *Love* INSIDE

WYND PRINCESS

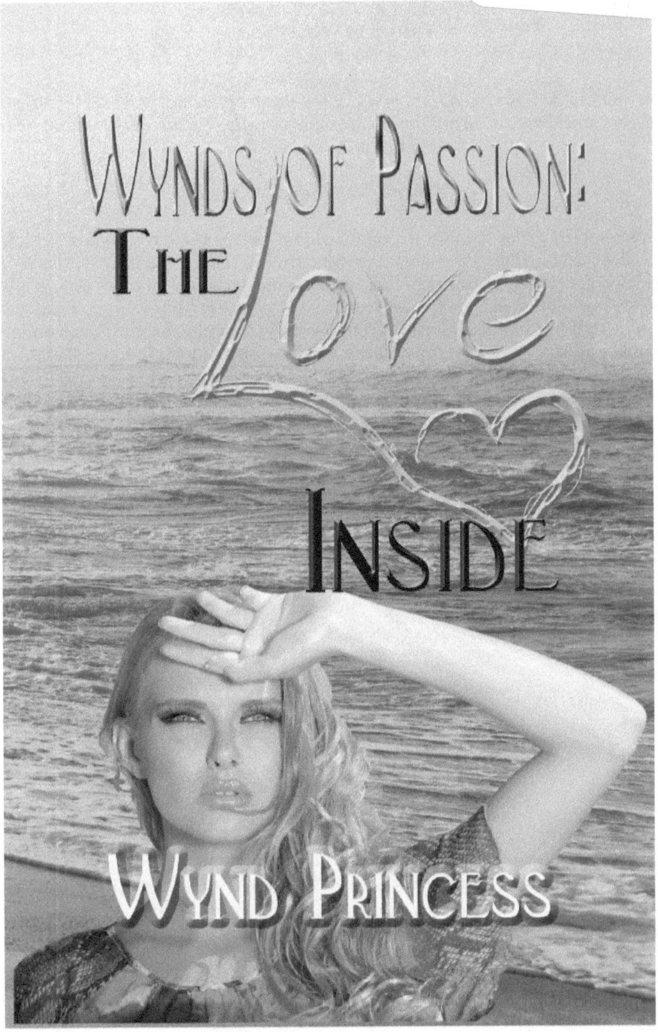

Wynd Princess

Wynds of Passion: The Love Inside
Written by Wynd Princess

Cover Designer: *Phoenix Publishing Associates*

Editor: *Phoenix Publishing Associates*

Formatter: *Phoenix Publishing Associates*

Wynds of Passion: The Love Inside

Wynd Princess

Table of Contents

PART One

Poems

8

Do You Believe

Do you believe in love at first sight?
I really didn't believe until I met you.
Deep down in my heart,
my love is eternal.
There are so many people in this world
that take advantage of another person's love,
and only use love to cause harm.

Is there any romance in this world anymore?
Romance is spending time with another,
just to be with them,
enjoy their company,
being close together.
Not how much money you can spend on
them.
Romance is not made of money,
I believe it is a feeling of joy and happiness
found only in the heart.

You need to show that person how deeply

Wynd Princess

you love them,
and how much you really do care.
Make each and every new day together
count.

Do You Love Me?

Do you still love me?
Or have you another?
It is not fair to lead me on.
Or tell me that you love me
when you really do not.

Do you miss me when I am not around?
I bet you do not even think of me.
Do you love me, yes or no?
Please do not say you do
when we both know you do not.

Do you know just how much I do love you?
In my heart, and in my soul?
But there are so many questions that remain.
Do you love me, yes or no?

Dream Dream Dream

Dream of me as you soon fall to sleep,
and all through the night.
Dream of me until the sun begins to shine,
and through the new day.

Wynds of Passion: The Love Inside

Dream or Reality

Have you ever seen a moonlight sky,
through the eyes of the person that you love?
Have you ever watched a beautiful sunset drift off
beyond a vast sea of blue?
Then after the sunset does disappear,
with it the sensual tide begins to roll in.
I begin to stroll in the slow-moving tide,
letting the brisk blue waters transcend across my
toes,
and across my supple feet and ankles.
I begin lightly kicking at the warm waters
that are up to my knees.
I looked up and saw you standing there,
right beside me.
You took my hand,
as we began to run through the night's tide.
We stopped, and from behind your back
you pulled out a very beautiful long stem pink
carnation,
trimmed in white.
I asked you what the carnation was for,
and you said just because you love me.

Wynd Princess

I closed my eyes, as you pulled me close
and kissed my ruby red lips.
Was I in a romantic dream?
Or did the night really happen?
Look down deep within your heart and your soul,
and I bet the answer is right in front of you.
Maybe the answer is in your dreams.

Wynds of Passion: The Love Inside

Forgive Me Lord

Forgive me Lord,
for there have been times in my life
where I have fallen short of your goodness and
glory.

Forgive me Lord.
Please open my eyes so that I may see
all your precious gifts you have giving to me.

Forgive me Lord,
give my life the love, and the strength, and the
glory,
so that my life may be lifted on high to be with you
eternally.

Forgive me Lord,
I know my life has taken wrong turns in the past.
Open my heart so I may find
the path that leads me straight to
the Pearly Gates of heaven, and to live with you.

Forgive me Lord.
Make my life a beacon, of light,
to show everyone that my life reflects you, and
Jesus Christ,

Wynd Princess

and that by excepting Jesus Christ into their hearts,
they, too, will live their life eternal.

Lord, let my words, and your light,
show the way through my everyday life.
Give me the voice to tell others of my testimony,
and maybe others will come to you through my
life.

He Caught My Eye

The man that I love is somewhat of a nut,
but that is what caught my eye.
He is very smart.
He really knows how to make a lady feel
she is all that and more.
For me, the love my husband does give,
is the true meaning of love.
I will always love, and cherish him forever, as time
will allow.
My husband Tully is a one in a million catch.

Just Listen

Listen, listen, listen.
Listen to all the sounds that the night can bring.
Listen to the sounds all around you.
Listen to the cars, and the trucks, passing on the
street.
Listen to the birds chirping their songs
to wake us up in the morning.
If you close your eyes,
I bet you can imagine the sounds
on a golden beach of your dreams.
Listen to the sounds of the seagulls
splashing in the sea for their food,
or picking up the leftovers on the sands.

If only we would stop, and listen,
to all the sounds of this world,
or in the sky,
maybe we could see things in a different light.
So, just listen.

Wynd Princess

Look to the Heavens

Look to the Heavens.
Watch the stars as they twinkle ever so bright.

Look to the Heavens.
See just how bright the moon can be.

Look to the Heavens.
Are the stars shining just for you?

Look to the Heavens.
Can you see a face on the moon?

Look to the Heavens.
The face that you will see,
is the man of your dreams.
Believe as long as there is a man upon the heavens,
the man of your dreams will be waiting
to make all of your dreams come true again.

Love and Honor For Robert

The freedom of this country
is because of men like you.
Men who fought for this land,
that we now can call home.
For our freedom you gave your life,
and now you live in the house of the Lord.
You feel no more pain, and no more sorrow.
I would like you to know
how much I do love you, Robert.
I am very proud to call you my brother,
and you always held up your country in high
respect.
You always knew that someday this country would
be free
for everyone to call home.
So, in your eyes, it made everything worth fighting
for.
I always love, and honor you.
Someday I know we will be together again,
behind those pearly gates of Heaven,
living in the house of our Father.

Our Friendship Will Grow

I am laying here in my bed,
just wondering to myself how you are,
and how you feel. You are just so far away.
I cannot just pick up the phone and give you a call,
because you are across the sea, in a totally
different land.
I was so happy when we first met on the computer.
I always looked forward to talking to you daily,
and seeing your face across my screen.
I knew that our friendship would grow day by day,
even though we were thousands of miles apart,
across the vast sea.
As time went on, and the days flew by,
I knew that our friendship would be everlasting.
I am really glad that I met somcone like you,
a down to earth man who is truly loved by all,
especially by me.

28

My Sweet Angel Dove

The sun begins to fade away,
beyond the warm waters of the sea.
The gentle tide caressing my feet,
persuading me to stroll in the waters,
before they gently collide with the sands upon the
shore.
I close my eyes.
I begin to wish that you again were by my side,
again, together our hearts will be one,
and our souls will be free.
Look up to the Heavens,
watch for that special star
that shines down on a clear night,
or brightly shine through the darkest evening sky.
I will be always be with you.
My sweet angel dove!

Seas Apart

You really are a great friend,
even though we have never really met.
We have met on the net,
but that is as far as it has gone.
Our friendship has lasted through thick and
thin,
even though we are a sea apart.
It is true, our friendship has grown over the
phone,
and over the net, and our special friendship
has lasted many years,
but I wish that friendship could blossom in
person.
Yes, our friendship is a special one,
and one I really hope never to lose,
I just wish we were together in the same
place,
and could go out and see each other face to
face.
Even though we are miles apart, across the
seas,
I do still love you and I always will.

Something to Think About

Has there ever been a time
when you felt that your life was worthless?
Where you feel your totally useless
and maybe a little confused?
It seems that you try to hold your head up high,
and try everything to stay above water,
but that is hard to do.
Sometimes it feels like I just give too much to
others,
and save nothing for myself.
At times, I feel like I am digging a hole for myself,
and everyone is happy to help throw the dirt over
me.
I have to keep trying,
I have to keep pushing forward,
and never look back.
Am I trying too hard to impress others?
You need to impress yourself first before you can
impress others.

Stop, Watch, and Listen

Listen to the sounds
of the whispering pines,
as they sway in the breeze.
Listen to the birds,
as they slip onto the branches.
If you really are quiet,
you can see the deer
frolicking through the woods.
The bunnies are diving into their rabbit holes,
making their squeaky sounds of joy.
There is a thin stream
running through the trees,
and around the rocks.
There is a walking trail through the woods,
with benches along the way,
so, you can sit there and watch
and listen to all the wildlife.
The sun shines through the trees,
and is beautiful to watch the different colors of the
sunset,
changing through each part of the pines.
The power of nature is a powerful thing,
it can stop your anxiety, depression, and relieve
stress.

So, take your time next time and stop, watch, and listen.

Teddy Bear and a Ring

It is sunset out now.
I can see all the pretty colors in the sky.
I can see outside my window in the front room.
I also can see the moon, and the stars trying to
come out.
I thought that I would take a walk along the sandy
beach
that happens to be in my back yard.
I can see the seagulls searching for food along the
beach
that people left there.
The gulls diving into the water for the fish they
like so much.
I walked down to the water's edge,
and strolled into the water, into the evening tide.
I heard a man clear his throat
So, I stopped and looked behind me to see who it
was,
and there he stood with his hands behind his back.
It was the man of my dreams.
He reached out from behind his back,
looked deep into my eyes and kissed me.
Then he handed me a long stem carnation.

Wynd Princess

Holding the flower was a teddy bear.
In the teddy bears paws was
a silver ring with red stones all around it,
and he placed it on my finger.
He said this ring is a symbol of my love for you.
Charlotte, will you marry me?
What do you think I said?
Hell yes! Hell yes, I will!
If you did not see what I said, here it is again.
Hell yes, I will!

Turmoils and Fears

Whenever you feel lonely, or feeling blue,
and you feel that no one really cares…
Just remember in me you have a friend.

When you feel the problems of the world
are weighing you down…
Just remember in me you have a friend.

Some people say that life is like a bowl of cherries.
Well, they forgot to tell us about the pits!
If life is a ray of sunshine, why does it rain?

There will be times in your life
when nothing is going your way.
You just want to break away…
Just remember in me you have a friend.

The Power of a Dream

Close your eyes and just relax.
Let your mind just fade into the abyss.
Think about that special place in your heart,
where the plush, rolling meadows of the green.
A place where the birds are always singing.
The trees are slowly swaying in time.
There is a rainbow forming over a small, peaceful
pond.
The deer begin to romp, and play, on the grassy
banks.

Sleep now, slumber now awaits.
Dream of me, and I will be there.
I will be waiting under an apple tree,
waiting for my angel to come
stir the embers of my heart.
Together, we both can ride upon that wonderful
rainbow,
and find our own pot of gold,
and make our dreams all come true.

There is Love Inside You

Love is truly a wonderful feeling.
Without feeling love,
you would soon shrivel up and die.
Then we would be all alone.
Love is never an easy feeling to have,
this I will admit.
You really have to work at love
for that feeling to blossom and really grow.
Sometimes love does have its ups and downs,
but if you do truly love another,
then that love will find a way
to reach out and touch another's heart.
Love is very important in someone's life,
just as much as water is.
You need to love yourself
before you can love someone else.
Give them your heart and your soul.
Love can be a very vibrant feeling,
but remember love can also destroy life and
dreams.
If the love that you feel is given to someone
special,
that love will become fruitful as each day passes
by.
When you are in love, your spirit becomes alive

and on fire.
It should never be pushed on anyone.
Always be faithful, and truthful
with that special someone,
If you do, believe me you will get
that special love in return.

This is What is Wrong

I know you have been wondering just what is
wrong,
and why my attitude has changed as of late.
Sometimes I do feel so alone, even when you are
around.
I have this feeling of emptiness way deep down
inside my heart, and in my soul.
I really try to make it look like I am happy,
and like nothing is wrong.
I hate to tell you, but the light in my heart is
growing dim.
I feel like there is a lump in my stomach.
I do not know how to get rid of it.
Are you trying to push me out of your life?
I really feel like you truly are.
Sometimes I do get upset, and I do not know why.
It is just that you make me feel like I am defective
at times.
In my mind, I begin to wonder if you do want
another.
You may say that you do not want another,
but your actions tell me something different.
Now, I realize why you do not want me around as
much.

Together Forever

Touch me.
Let me feel the warmth of your skin
pressed against mine.
Embrace me.
I need to feel the warmth of sweet body
wrapped all around me.
Kiss me.
Press your tender lips
against my sweet, supple lips.
Make love to me.
Slowly and oh so gently,
let our bodies become as one.
Feel our hearts touch one another.
Let our bodies heat grow stronger and stronger,
as our bodies sway together.
I truly hope with all my heart
we will always be together
for as long as time will allow.
May our love last within our hearts
and within our souls, forever more.

Tonight Belongs to Us

If I ask you to follow me, will you?
If I ask your heart to dance with me, will it?
Follow me to our special place,
where the silvery sands meet
the dark blue waters of the evenings tide.
Dance with me under the glow of the golden
moon,
and move to the twinkling of the stars.
There is a silence, and calmness of the sea.
Let the night totally engulf our hearts, and our
souls.
Let our bodies intertwine on the still
warm sands of the night,
Our spirits will always live as one, never to part.
May our love be filled with all the passion that two
people can possess,
and may that passion possess our hearts, and souls.
May that special love never be broken.

50

Torn

How can I let you know
that all the feelings I had for you have now
changed?
It is not easy for me to tell you
just how I really feel.
I know deep down inside
that I really do not want to leave you.
Yet, to be painfully honest,
things between us just are not working out.
The one thing I do know,
is that I do always want to be your friend.
I know that a lot of the problems
we have had were my fault.
Still, I also know that I have changed towards you.
There were things that you have said and done
that have really hurt me.
Yes, I still do love you and I always will,
but I feel that the love I hold is now more of as a
friend.
My fairy tale dream has now turned into a
nightmare,
but maybe that nightmare will turn around.

Wynd Princess

Watching Over Mother Earth

May the spirits of the elders that once lived on
Mother Earth,
show us peace, love, and happiness.
Let them show us how to live off the land.
How to make clothing just the way they did.
Show us how to cook the way they did.
To make shelter wherever they may have been.
Most of all we need to learn to give thanks
for all Mother Earth has provided for us.
Let not things the elders of the nation be
overlooked,
or even just forgotten.
The natives only killed what they needed.
They did not kill anything for sport
Why can we not learn from the native nation?
I think that we should go back to nature as it
should be.

What Happened to Our Love?

What is wrong with me?
Why can I not find love?
It seems that I cannot ever do
anything right in the eyes of a man.
Since I have changed my life around for the better,
it seems that you believe that I have not changed,
and that my life is all made up.
It also seems that no matter how hard I try,
things with you and I will never be the same.

I know there is someone else that touches your
heart,
that I definitely do not.
Sometimes you feel very distant from me,
even though you say you are not.
If I just talk to you or even joke around,
I am trying just too hard,
but it feels like I am chasing you away, even as a
friend.

I know I am not giving you what you want
in a lover, a wife, or a friend.
So now there is another who is taking my place,
and that is not easy to handle.
I am not saying that the love you once felt is

totally gone.
I am just saying that the love that we once felt for
one another
will never be again.

With My Mind's Eye

With my mind's eye,
I see the world the way god intended it to be.

With my mind's eye,
I see a world with no more sorrow, or pain.

With my mind's eye,
I see mankind treating others with kindness.

With my mind's eye,
I see no more gangs, no more fighting,
with means no more wars.

With my mind's eye,
I see mankind treating our war veterans
with the respect that they do justly deserve.

With my mind's eye,
I see the world with no more fears.

With my mind's eye,
I see others helping the homeless,
by giving them warmth,
and a place to sleep or stay and food.

Wynd Princess

With my mind's eye,
I see others helping the children of this world,
before helping the children of foreign countries.

With my mind's eye,
the world is a much safer, brighter,
and healthier place to live.

How do you see this world in your mind's eye?

You Can Always Change

People with an addiction are hooked on a powerful
drug.
No matter if it is a street drug, given by a Dr., or
even alcohol.
Drugs will take over your life, body, heart, and,
soul.
You will do anything to get your next fix, your
next drink.
Drugs will take away your family,
and even your real friends.
You will develop those false relationships
with the ones who can keep you hooked.
You will even sell anything you can,
even your life's possessions, or heirlooms,
just to get that next high, or drink.
Once you are a person with an addiction,
you will always be a person with an addiction.
Only you can change your own life.
Yes, you do need the help of those professionals,
and your family.
Believe me, you can do it
if, and only if, you, yourself, wants to change for
you.
Get help. You can't do it alone. Take that first
step.

You Are Not Perfect

My love for you has all but vanished.
You broke my heart,
and tore my soul apart,
as you took your love from me.
You act as if a person's love flows just like water,
as if it were flowing through a faucet.
To be able to turn on and off as they please.
To me you took the cowards way out.
You never said you wanted to work things out
between us.
You never said a thing to me.
Only stomped on my love as if it were trash.
When I asked you why your love for me is now
gone,
you never admitted that you did anything wrong.
The only thing that you did say
was that you no longer loved me,
but with no reason why.
I must face the facts.
You're not, and never were, or never will be,
the "perfect man" that you think you were or
maybe,
that you think you still are.

Wynd Princess

Your Beautiful Face

As the breeze blows,
and starts to sing through the leaves and the
bushes,
the sweet sunset drifts slowly across the sea of
blue.
I look beyond the swaying trees,
and there is the silvery beach.
The evening tide splashes across the rocks
in the place where the waters of the sea
meets the cool sands of the beach.
I walk down the beach, take off my shoes and
socks,
and slide the waters, and the sand, through my
toes.
I see the first star of the night, and I make a wish.
I wish for the man that I do love to be by my side,
and sweep me off my feet.
If a man does come to you,
then yes, he is the man of your dreams.
Even if it is someone different
than your heart feels passion for.
If you do make a heartfelt and sincere plea
on that special first star,

I bet that the right man will soon appear.
Then together your love will forever see you
through.

Part Two
Prose

Back to the Light

How come the world is in such turmoil and destruction? People just seem not to care. There is just too much death between more and more people. Some of these people just do not care at all.

Put the Lord first and your life will soon be in alignment. Put the Lord first and his light will shine through you.

Too many people in the world do not believe in the Lord. They think their life now is totally up to them. People think that doing as they please nothing wrong can happen. They believe their lives are untouchable.

Put the Lord first and your life will soon be in alignment. Put the Lord first and his light will shine through you.

In today's world, life is in the very tough times. With drugs, and shootings you do not know what to do. Most people stay in their homes, afraid they will be shot through a drive by, either accident, or just by being in the way.

We need to put the world back into the light.

Church

Why do I feel like this? I am really hurt.
I guess I try too hard to please some people, but I just feel that they take advantage of that, they just seem to walk all over me. One the thing is that I guess I just am not good enough just to be a good friend. People never say Good job Charlotte, or I am glad you're there for me, or Hey you are doing a great job. Or even just a thanks, or even 'We know you don't have to the things that you do for us, but we want you to know we thank you very much'.

Nope.

Believe me, other people can get that recognition. Some can even be formally appreciated by their names, announced to all. I just really hurt because I try so hard, and I do not get that recognition. Sometimes I feel like I am not shown any thanks at all, because some people automatically think that I will always be there to fall back on. I would never leave anyone in the dark.

Wynds of Passion: The Love Inside

I do not ever want to say anything because I am afraid I will be replaced, like a light bulb that can be replaced when it blows. Or like changing your clothes.

I get 'oh she is always smiling when she is at church', 'we all love seeing Charlotte at the sanctuary door passing out the bulletins, and greeting everyone good morning'.

I know this sounds petty huh, but I do work hard there and even give my input to make things better for the church. I even volunteer to make dishes for events.

Maybe I should not complain, but this month was Pastor appreciation month. Other volunteers were asked to make a video about both of our Pastors. Some of them have been volunteering as long as I have, some not even as long.
Sometimes I just feel invisible.

Guess I just do not understand. I try, I really do, but I guess I am just a nobody in the church.
Except to Jesus Christ our Lord, and of course my husband, I am just a nobody.

Disabled I Am Not

Disabled I am not.

Yes, my left leg was amputated from just above the knee, but I am still the same lady I always was and will forever be.

Disabled I am not.

People need to see me for the strong person that I am, not the poor girl that they think I am, or should be.

Disabled I am not.

Yes I do still need help at times, but I have never given up on myself. The Lord still has a plan for my life here in this world, and there are people here who love and care for me. I will not let them down, ever.

Disabled I am not.

Wynds of Passion: The Love Inside

To my husband, I am as beautiful as I ever was if not more now, even with only one leg.

Disabled I am not.

The world does not owe me a thing, just because I am labeled as disabled, or handicapped.

If you feel sorry for me, or even look down upon me because I only have one leg, then you never were my friend at all.

Just because I only have one leg, I have never changed. No, my personality is now the same as it was before. I might have felt low at one point, but what can you expect. When I did feel low, there were two people who set me straight, and they were God and his son, Jesus Christ.

Just because I only have one leg, does not mean that the world has ended.

There are still people who need me in their lives, as much as I need them. I even have a cat named Mala, who needs me to be around. I need her just as much.

A true friend loves you for the person that you are. Not for the person that they can cold into what they want you to be!

Do not be scared of me, and do not run away, and please throw me no "pity parties". Just treat me like a human being. Treat me the same way that you would like to be treated, the way you believe you deserve to be treated.

75

Give Yourself Time

Have you ever watched a sunset reflect on a sea of blue? A sea where the winds above do not seem to blow, and the waters below are very calm, as if they were made of glass. The deep colors of the sunset reflect the colors of the rainbow above.

Listen to the sounds of the seagulls, as they dive into the waters below for their food.

Feel the silky sands at the tides end, as you walk in the place where the waters meet the land. Feel the warm waters as it rolls over your feet, and back again into the sea.

Remember when you are working, or if you are at home and everything is falling in all around you, just stop, and take some time out for yourself. Whether it is on a white sandy beach, or with your family. Just take that time to relax and remember that there is a special place that you can go to and have fun.

77

Going In Circles

Why does it feel like my life is going round and round in circles that are never ending? At times I feel like my life has finally stopped spinning, and something sets me back.

Sometimes, I sit here and wonder if I should just say everything I do, every pain I have, and every thought that I have, is in the hands of my Lord. At times I do wonder if I am just pushing too hard. Maybe I need to close my eyes and say – after I take a deep breath – things will happen as they may. So, I told myself to just stop stressing and just go with the flow.

I am ashamed to be living in a world like what we have today. Everyone is just killing others for stupid reasons, or you are caught in the line off fire just because someone is trying to shoot someone else and you are standing in the way. There is drugs in this world that people are killing for, or weapons, even in just plain revenge, or payback!. Some people kill just because you looked at them wrong.

The Native Americans of old looked greatly upon

this earth. They nurtured the land that is called mother earth. They gave back to mother earth by planting foods and herbs. The Natives of old killed only what they needed, and nothing more. Every part of an animal was used for food, or clothing, or weapons, or shoes, even shelter. They never killed for sport. The birds such as the eagle, or the hawk, or the bear or the wolf, were very sacred to them. They believed that they were part of the animal they choose to be.

So why do we feel so lonely, so confused in this world? Why can we not learn from the Native Americans of old? Treat this Earth as if she will never fade away.

Still I feel I am missing something. Something God has planned for my life. To give back to Mother Earth, nurture the Earth, and let things grow.
All I know is not to faulter in my life, let the things that I am destined for in life just happen.

If I think about it, my life has been blessed. I was born with epilepsy. I had grandmal seizures. The doctors and the nurses did not know if I would even survive, but here. I am fifty-five years old, and I am doing fine. I wonder what would have happened in the day of our elder Native Americans. I wonder if I would have survived. The elder Native Americans were close to God, and Mother Earth. Sometimes I think that Native Americans had a closer faith than many people do today.

Today I am a published author. I would love the doctors, and the nurses, even certain teachers from elementary school, all the way through high school to see how accomplished I am today. To know that I could do it. My mother never gave up on me. She helped me with flash cards, pictures of different problems, riding a bike, just everything. My mother even worked with me therapy wise, and speech wise, when no one else would. They thought I would never have a productive life so why should they even try with me. They thought it would be a waste of time and money.

You can do anything that you put your mind to, and push yourself, no matter what other people think, or no matter what life throws at you. Just remember… You can do it! Don't ever say you can't!

Some say I am disabled, but it is just mentally challenged to me. I never will say I am handicapped. Do not feel sorry for yourself. Did the Native Americans feel jealousy? No, they never had to feel that emotion. Always live your life one day at a time, but with a passion that only you can possess.

Wynd Princess

Halloween Night

What does Halloween really mean?
Most children believe Halloween means scary
stories, candy, and dressing up in costumes to go
trick or treating. Even carving pumpkins, and
hanging out scary things, or listening to scary
music.

Do you know what Halloween really means?
The real name is All Hallows Eve. Legend says
that this is the night where the sprits of the dead do
arise and are allowed to roam the earth for one
night.

Some women in Salem were proclaimed as
witches or they were self-proclaimed witches, and
they were burned at the stake, or even hung by
their neck until dead.

Decide for yourself what is true or false, then you
can believe what you will.

Wynd Princess

His Love Will Shine Through

The day is dark, snowy, and cold, but there is
someone who warms my heart, and soul. The
person I am talking about died on the cross for our
sins. He sits on the right hand of his father, behind
the pearly gates of Heaven.
My warmth comes from the love I have for Jesus
Christ, our Lord and Savior. I have taken our
Lord's love, that he holds for me, into my heart,
have you?

Our lords love stems deep into my soul, and warms
me through and through.
Our heavenly father does love us no matter what.
His love is unconditional.
If you have not taken the love of Jesus Christ into
your heart, now is the time. Your life can start
anew. You will soon see, that the love of our Lord
and Savior, Jesus Christ, is already inside of you.
Your eyes just need to open to that love.

Open your heart, and you will see the love for
Christ will shine through and through.

In My Mind's Eye

In my mind's eye, I can see the world the way it should be. With no war, no drugs, and even every person in this world gets along. No matter what color they are. No matter what nationality they are. No matter what religion they are.

In my mind's eye, I see a world with no pain, no sorrow, and no fear. Only happiness. Everyone loves the Lord and has taken Jesus into their hearts.

In my mind's eye, I can see men, women, and children, are treating each other with love and respect.

In my mind's eye, I can see a government that takes care of our countries children first. That gives them the health care that they need, and makes sure our children are all feed with nutritional food in their bellies, and clothes on their backs, and shoes and socks on their feet.

In my mind's eye, I also see a government that listens to the people, and makes changes in the laws to abide by people's hopes. Maybe we all can agree to be as one. A president, and a congress, who are for the people, not themselves. Keeping SSI and food stamps, for the people who need them.

In my mind's eye, I see more people giving their lives to our Lord and Savior, Jesus Christ. Living their lives for the Lord, and professing to others their love for him, and the promise of eternal life.

In my mind's eye, over all I see the world as a kinder, safer, and healthier place to live.

What can you see in your mind's eye?

Wynd Princess

In the Eyes of the Lord

What is wrong with the world today, I just do not understand why there is so much fighting, and so much wars.

In the Bible it says, to love all mankind. It does not say anything about God picking and choosing any one mankind. The Lord does love one man, women, or child over another.

Does not the Lord say, to love thy neighbor? That means, love thy fellow man, no matter their nationality, or race, or their creed, color, or religion, or even if they are rich or poor.

Why can the world not get together, and be all of Gods children in our eyes like it is in the Lord's. The world was never meant to have pain, and suffering.

Man was created in the image of the Lord, Jesus Christ. I really wish it could be the way things were meant to be once again.

Wynd Princess

Let Us Become One

See me.
Look deep into my eyes and see the person, the
lady that I truly am, and the true friend that I hope
I am. NOT just a friend, or a "fake" friend, but a
true friend, the person I am now.

Touch me.
Feel the softness of my skin, feel all the curves that
my body holds. I want to feel your hands, and your
lips, upon my tender skin. Please let me feel your
sweet male member, opening, and entering my
sweet flower, over and over again.

Kiss me.
Press your tender lips against my lips. Let me feel
your lips caressing every inch of my body.

Let our bodies, our hearts, and our souls always be
held as one, and never shall they part.

Love vs True Love

Some people say that the word love means to never have to say you're sorry. I think they are wrong. If you truly are in love, if you are wrong, and you know it, saying you're sorry is a sign of true love. If the saying that being in love never means you have to say 'I am sorry' was true, then would that not be playing with a person's emotions? With their heart? How could you ever believe that those words were coming from a person's soul?

If you were married, and your husband or your wife told you that they truly loved you, but yet had an affair on you, could they just say I am sorry, and expect everything to be ok? Could you say without a shadow of a doubt that the love was real? If you were truly in love, your spouse would never have an affair on you. So, you would have no reason to doubt them at all.

Yet, some people use the term 'I love you' only to get what they want from another, then toss them out with the trash. They might wine and dine you, bring you flowers and/or candy, but they are wanting that end result no matter what you want. They say I did all this for you, now what will you do for me? They might even call you names and label you with their friends as being easy.

Is love just a tool, or something to be played with? Like a toy?
The internet says there really is no difference between true love and love, only how the words are said. I beg to differ. If you truly love someone, you will do anything for them – within reason of course – and you want to spend the rest of your life with them. You want to give them your heart and soul That person is your soul mate as well as your best friend. You know that when they say the words 'I love you', that they are coming from their heart.

If you truly love someone, you want to tell your partner your most inner thoughts. You want to be honest with them. You want that special person in every part of your life no matter how fantastic that part of your life is, or how ugly it is. You want them to know all about your past, present, and future.

You might find your soul mate in high school, in college, in church, or maybe when you just are not even looking for anyone at all. Believe me, that special person is out there just for you, he or she is out there somewhere in this great big world, just waiting for you.

Wynd Princess

Men vs Women

Most men feel that they are the superior ones. That most women are the weak and weary ones, but baby, nothing could be farther from the truth.
In most cases men and women are meant to be equals. No one is meant to be the bigger ones, towering over one another.

Men say that they are better than women because men do not show their emotions as women do. Women show their emotions at the drop of a hat and wear their emotions on their sleeves. Men do have emotions, they just mainly hold them in, keep them to themselves.

Yes, it is true that, at times, women do need help from men. However, at times, men do need help from women as well.

So, do not say you are better than I, or that I am wrong for showing my emotions, or that I am weak.

My friend, I believe it is you that is wrong!

95

Wynd Princess

Miss Dianne's Wedding Vows

I, Miss Dianne Marie, have waited many days and nights for you to come to the United States, and to me, and my family. The love that I have found in you will forever be.

I fell in love with your strength, your sweet voice on the computer, and in your golden wit, and in your special charm. When I finally saw you, the man that I fell in love with, my love grew even stronger.

The Lord on high had a special plan for us. Today, that is coming true.
If and only if you do agree to accept the angelic gifts that I now present.

I do promise to be your forever bride. I now do present to you my three angels in my life – Ashley Irene, Kristine Lee and Victoria Marie.

I give you this ring, with the promise of my everlasting love.

Wynd Princess

Mr. Sexy Man

From the first time I met you, I had this very at ease feeling about you. I knew that you were the kind of man who had a special quality about himself, and a man who could always make someone smile, even on that person's worst of days.

A man who had a stern side to himself when the time called for it, but a man who could also turn tempers around, and make things better again. Even if you had a trying day at work, you always went home with a smile.

You, Bob, and my best friend Crystal, are very special people, friends, and family, and that very special couple. You both made me feel kind of envious because the two of you had such a warm, and loving relationship, and not many people can say that.

Your family opened up your doors to me, after sis and I had met online, and each of you made me feel warm, welcome, and at home.

So, Bob, you will be very missed, but we know that you are in a better place now. A place where pain, and fear do not exist. A place where you are sitting with our Lord and Savior. In fact, I tend to believe that you are sitting on high, telling jokes and laughing.

I know you would not want anyone to grieve over you, for you will again reunite with your loving family, and their loved ones behind the pearly gates.

So hold on to your smile, and the laughter, and you will never again frown.

My Dear Rodney

Life is not a dream, but a painful reminder of how cruel people can be. In a split seconded anyone's life could be taken away, or yet a person's life could slowly – sometimes even painfully – be taken.

To me, you were – and still are – that special man that I love. You were the one who could always make me laugh, and always brought a smile to my face. You were a very gentle hearted man, and someone who would always helped others. Yet, if the time arose for you to have a stern heart and hand, you were the one who could deliver.

You really loved life. You loved it when we went places together just to relax. Maybe life did not accept us as a couple, but that never bothered you at all. It did me, but you calmed me down, and brought that smile back to my face.

You always gave as much of yourself as you possibly could to me, as I to you. You helped others to see a light when they thought no light was at the end of their tunnel. Rodney, I have no doubt that you are in a better place right now. A place where no one cares how you lived your life, no one cares if you were gay, or straight. I bet right now, you are sitting on high in Heaven telling all kinds of jokes.

I know that if I turned my eyes to the sky, that you will be watching over me until the time I am with you again.

Love always and forever, Randy.

My Forever Love

It is nearly sunset now over our special beach. The colors of the sun fill the sky. As the sun is fading away, the moon, and the stars, are now starting to appear. The gentle slow waters of the tide rise upon the golden sands. The waters of the evenings look so calm, they have the image of smooth glass. There I begin to stroll in the cool waters. The tide tickling my toes in the sands awaiting for the time the man of my dreams that I do love comes to be with me on the beach, until the sun begins to shine.

As I stood upon the sands, I reached into my pocket. Then I took my cell phone out, and thought I would call my love at his work, and tell him that I loved him, and I always will. I knew he was ready to get off work, and he would be on his way.

He told me on the phone that he had a VERY important, life changing question to ask me. He said that he was on the road now, and would be here very soon.

Then through the phone, I heard a very loud crash. I screamed and shouted his name, but I got no answer. Finally, the phone had gone dead.

Later that night my love's best friend had come to the beach to find me. He had told me that the crash I had heard on the phone was his phone hitting the floor, because my love had hit a semi-tractor, and had died in the ambulance. I dropped to my knees and put my hands over my mouth and just started screaming, 'No! No! No! This cannot be. He is alive, I know it. He has to be alive. You have to be wrong! He is alive I know he is!'

On the way to the hospital, he took my hand and placed a box in my hand. 'He made me promise to come find you, give it to you, and to tell you that you will ALWAYS be his forever love.'

It seems that I heard the police say that the semi driver was found to be heavily drunk. An open bottle of Patron was found beside his body in the cab. He was taken to the hospital, and is in a coma, and his chances do not look good at all to survive the crash.

Through heavy tears, I took the box and opened it. Inside was a small ceramic kitten with a ring tied around its neck. In the bottom of the box was a note, that he had written to me when he was in the ambulance. It said, "Will you marry me?" I slipped the ring on my finger. It was the ring I had seen in a small shop in a little town that we had stopped in to have lunch. The tears fall harder down my cheeks.

I heard his voice coming from the Heavens. I looked up, and in a cloud, I happened to see a face clear as a bell. It was my fiancé. He said to me, 'Yes, baby, I am now in Heaven. So, dry your tears. I have no more pain.
Whenever you are weary, or really depressed, or just need to talk, just look to the Heavens, and I will be there. I am that bright shining star, even on the darkest of nights. As long as you believe in me, I will always be here, right here with you. You will forever be my baby. This I hope you know, but I have to go now. I will be waiting here for you, until the day we can be together again.' Then my love was gone, but I was not sad anymore, because he will always be with me.

Someday, together our souls will touch, and we'll be together again.

105

Wynd Princess

My Knight in White Satin

Many a night I sit in my apartment all alone,
waiting for my knight in white satin to ride up. To
take me away from all the killings and problems.
All the drugs, in this world.

I sit and wait for my knight in shining armor to
take me to paradise. Where never again is there
sickness, or words can never hurt. A place the
flowers are always in bloom, and they are every
color that Mother Earth can make.
There are fields of green all around us, and trees
large and small everywhere the eye can see.
Streams of ice blue waters filled with plenty of
motley color fish everywhere.

I really wish my knight in white satin would come
and sweep me off my feet, and take me away. Take
me to a land of perfection and dreams, but I know
that no such place exists. My knight will never
come.

When you're a child, you have dreams of a big
wedding, with a fantastic dress, the best wedding

your imagination could come up with.
A flower girl, a ring bearer, bridesmaids, and
everything done in their favorite color.

What did you dream of?

One Day at a Time

I wish that we could have just one more
chance to have a life together. I really want
to give you the love that I once felt for u
again. The love that I felt down deep in my
heart and soul, and receive that love from
your heart again.

I would let the love become strong naturally,
not rush into things as I did before. I would
take one day at a time. Never would I want
you to make any promises that I know you
cannot keep, and those promises would be
held strong.

I would like you to promise me one thing.
Can you promise me that the love that you
feel will never roam to another? Maybe
someday you may let me into your heart,
and into your soul.
Please believe me when I say to you that the

love I feel is only for you. The love I give to you is nothing but very strong and will forever be yours.

Wynd Princess

Our Special Night

Come with me into my peaceful dream world, where our souls will be one, and never part. Let us walk hand in hand, barefoot in the warm waters of the evenings tide, rolling upon the silvery sands of time. Splashing each other just like we were kids again, playing in the waters of our souls.

Together we begin to dance, dance to the waters of the night. We dance to the tide crackling on the rocks. The waters are flowing upon the cool sands. We dance in the moonlight, and to all the twinkling stars, reflecting bright colors upon the sea.

We fall into each other's arms and fall upon the shore. The waters ripping around our bodies. He takes off my long, wet, black dress, and my panties, and throws them upon the shore. Then he takes off his shirt and pants.

We lay in each other's arms, as we passionately kiss, and run our hands up nnd down each other's bodies. He grabs one breast, then the other, and slightly pinches and pulls them both, turning me on big time! I raise my head, and nibble on his lips. Sucking them, biting them, then very seductively licking them.

His hands moved slowly down my body, making me hotter than ever. Even the cool waters could not cool us down. He pushed my legs apart. His finger slide inside my pulsating pink pearl, as he stroked himself, getting ready to enter me. He removed his fingers and pressed his enormous member inside of my pink pearl. Slow at first, but then his hips began to move faster and faster to the movement of the tide.

After we were done making love, we moved our hot bodies farther into the cool waters to wash ourselves off. By that time our clothes were pretty dry, so we walked onto the sands and we got dressed. Back to reality! Back to this unfriendly world, but we will always have our special night!

Playing Games with Love

Love is not a game. So, why do most people treat it like it is? They treat love as if it was a toy. Most men use it as a tool to get what they want. Then they just throw the woman away like the trash.

Do you feel that love is so much more? Love is much more than a word, but a feeling. A feeling on so many levels. Love takes time to find, to cultivate and grow. When you do find love, it takes so much time and work to keep alive.

Love is something special, deep down in your heart, in your soul. It is a joy, a warmth that you feel that you can share with another. Before you can give your love to another, you need to love yourself. Do not push love on anyone, if it was meant to happen then it will happen, even if it takes a little time.

If only you're in love, well, that love was not meant to happen at all. When love, I mean true love happens to come along, then both of your hearts will know it, and you will never want to share your hearts, or souls, with anyone else. True love is unconditional. Once you find that love, you will never part.

Wynd Princess

Single or Married in the Church

Usually on a Sunday, I never feel alone and powerless, but I did today. This morning our associate Pastor Mrs. Becky Jones Crain gave the sermon. The topic was singles in the church. Truthfully, Pastor Becky did a fantastic job, but I have never felt so alone, and powerless. When I left church, I was crying.

Some people in the church believe in being single, as their choice. Yet, the church believes that singles are taught as a stepping stone to the goal of marriage.

Some people know this. George Schoff and I were married, but because we could not live on just his social security check, I was allowed to draw a social security check but the bare minimum. We could not live even on that, so we were told that we HAD to get a divorce. I even had to move out so I would have my own address. That was the only way we could pay our rent.
Now, we both live in the same apartment buildings, but a couple of doors down from each

other.
I talked to my Pastor, Pastor Nate, and he researched it legally since we were told we had to divorce. We both thought, in our hearts, we believed that we were still married, then, in the eyes of God, we were still married.

Everyone is a child of the Lord, and we did not want to do anything wrong in his eyes. If you think that you are not a child of God, then you live your life the way you think you should. As a child of God, then we do not want to break his laws of how marriage should be in his eyes, and the way of the Bible.

With all my medical conditions, we had to pay a deductible of $300.00 before Medicaid would pay anything. Now, that has changed, since I am supporting myself.

Yes, our love is true. George is my soul mate, and that kind of love is rare. We would still be married legally if we did not have to get a divorce, that much is true. We will be married until the day that we die. This much is true, as well. So, now that we are still married in the eyes of the Lord, we feel closer to him.

Yes, I do know that everyone does have their own opinion. If they still do not believe me, then I encourage them to please talk to my Pastor. He and

Wynd Princess

Pastor Becky are very knowledgeable. I don't believe they would ever tell anyone anything that was not God's word. If they have questions about something that you have asked, they will look it up and sit with you and show you right in the Bible what it says. I have asked Pastor Nate many things about things about his sermons, because my granddad was a pastor before he died. I was a second grade Sunday school teacher in Las Vegas, as well as a seconded grade Sunday School teacher in California.

George's children are now grown, and so are my daughters. They have their own opinions. Truthfully, I do not think they really care what we think. His daughter is the only one of them that kind of understands. As long as her father is happy with me then that is all that really matters. His children really do not like me, though, and I really do not know why. Hey, it is not their life, is it?.

Single or married in the church should not matter because everyone, in the Lord's eyes, is the same. Some people have a gift from God of being single, some are given the gift of marriage. How we perceive Christ is how we should be perceived in the church, not if we are married or not!

Soldiers: Now and Past

This memorial day, we, the people, need to honor the men, and women, who diligently fought for this land that we call home. We honor not only the souls who have shed their blood, and or died for this great land. We also honor the families of the ones that have been left behind to live without their loved ones – husbands, wives, even their sons or daughters. The families still need to push on to start to again live their lives.

We need to teach our children how brave their father, mother, sister, or brother was. They need to know why the wars were fought. Why people got hurt or died. Our children need to know why our country is free.

Do not let us forget the soldiers of today. For their sacrifices that they have made. For the honor and glory, they have given to us. Just for all of this country to be free.

We also honor the parents who have adopted those innocent children of this war, so those children can go on and live their lives.

We need not forget our veterans of today. The sacrifices that they have made for all of the American people. We honored them during the time of war. So, is there a reason we do not honor them now? The soldiers today that fought in the Vietnam war or Hiroshima were labeled as "baby killers". So, now they are forgotten and disregarded as trash. They are forgotten, living in filth, on the streets, sick, hungry, and cold.

How can we, as Americans, knowing our freedom was won because of these men, treat our veterans this way. In God's eyes, they are no different than you and I are. What would you do if you were treated that way? Would you want to go hungry all the time, or live on the streets, or be dirty all the time, or cold? We need to cloth these men and women, give them jobs and not be prosecuted. Give them shelter not just when it is cold out, but all the time. A lot of these men live in card board boxes. We should give them good, wholesome foods, give them blankets, if there are no shelters that we can send them to. We need to be proud of these men, not treat them like monsters!

We expect certain things in life just to survive. Like health insurance when we are sick or hurt, but what if we did not have those things? What would you do? Some of our vet's do not expect things handed to them. They want to earn their way just like regular people, which, to me they are. There is no difference. We all are children of God, no matter if we are a different color, a religion, or a creed. Man, woman, or child, God sees everyone as the same.

So, remember anything can change. One day that person on the streets could be you. Or that person that has nothing to eat. You could be the person that is cold, or that is hurt or sick. Put yourself in the vet's place, and I am sure you will have a different outlook on life.

121

Something We Should Never Forget

People say love conquers all, but it is just not in the cards for everyone. Some people never find love, they do not love themselves, much less other people. The one person that not anyone can ever chase away, who loves us unconditionally is the Lord Jesus Christ.

Jesus Christ died for our sins. He did not pick and choose who he would love, or who he would save, or who he would let into heaven. All people have the chance to accept the Lord into their hearts and have everlasting life.

Our Lord's love, grace and prosperity is the same for every man, woman, and child. The Lord does not play favorites. Take me, for example. Just because I am missing my left leg from just above the knee, he does not love me any less then someone who has all body parts. Everyone is whole in God's eyes. So, why do we discriminate just because someone has a disability, or a body part that is missing?

Wynds of Passion: The Love Inside

I believe that there are people in this world that are wrestling with their faith. They do not see the light inside the tunnel. All they can see is the darkness. I, also, believe that God, the father, the creator of the Heavens and the Earth, will always show us the light every tunnel. All you have to do is open your eyes, and your heart, and believe.

The problem that most people have is that they think God is mad at them because of something they have done in their life. God does not get angry, or never takes revenge on anyone. Jesus is the truth and the light, and no one can get to the Father but through him. That is a promise we should always remember. The one saying we should never forget, over everything we hear, and everything we read. Never, ever, forget these words.

The Imagination of a Child

In the eyes of a child the world could very well be an adventure. They could be Captain Hook, fighting against the Lost Boys, and Peter Pan. Or a princess like Ariel, living under the sea with King Triton and Sebastian, or even Ursula the sea witch. Maybe even a swash buckling pirate like Blackbeard, in search for buried treasure. Could be even become the fair maiden Maid Marion waiting for her knight in shining armor to rescue her, and whisk her away from her prison, and her emotional chains.

A child has an imagination that can travel near, or to a faraway land. Anywhere, a child may go. They may become anyone that their mind can imagine. A child's heart is so open, so free, so innocent.

Some people say that a child's eyes are the portal to the soul. If that is true, then may a child's soul run free, and let their souls never know any sorrow or pain. May they live their younger years running like the wind to those places that take them to where their hearts can run rampant.

Just think, if our minds, and our souls could fly away anywhere we wanted to go, where would you go?

Wynd Princess

The Light of Heaven Awaits

Have you excepted the Lord as your personal
Savior?
Excepting Jesus Christ as your Lord and Savior
starts with a willing heart.
Love the Lord with all your heart and soul, and
never stop believing. Dare to love all thy neighbors
in his name.

The symbol of Baptism shows how your life is
beginning anew. Your life was full of sin, but after
you have arose from the purifying waters of the
Lord, your life is like brand new. You are a child
of Jesus Christ.

Jesus Christ died on the cross to dissolve us of our
sins, if only you believe.
Three days after Christ had died on the cross and
was buried in linen cloth, then sealed in his holy
tomb, Jesus arose out of his holy tomb, and
ascended to Heaven to sit on the right hand of His
father.

Your life is eternal if Jesus is in your heart. Jesus

will meet you at the pearly gates, and your life will be judged. Then Jesus Christ will assent and take you to be with His holy father.

Things to Think About

"If life is full of sunshine, and rainbows, then tell me this, why does it rain?"

"They say that life sucks, then you die. However, accept the Lord as your personal Savior, and the promise of eternal life shall be yours."

"People say that life is like a bowl of cherries, messed up and forgot to warn us about the pits".

"If life is supposed to be a box of chocolates, then why is life so bitterly sour?"

129

Wynd Princess

True Friends vs Fake Friends

True friends love you through thick and thin. They never give up on you. People who pretend to be your friend, but leave you in a time of trouble or need, truly are fake.

If you do something wrong, a true friend will help you. They will talk to you and say, 'hey, I think you're wrong, and this is why'.

A true friend is there to help you along the path that the Lord Jesus has for you. If you stray from that path, a true friend will help lead you back to the straight and narrow. If you have a problem, and it seems nothing is going your way, and you feel your life is going downhill, a true friend will be there right next to you, right by your side.

If you are in love, and the person you're in love with is a "trouble maker". If everyone can tell you just how bad this person is, yet you just do not want to listen. A true friend will help you to see the light.

Wynds of Passion: The Love Inside

A true friend will always be there to stand by you through all the good times, as well as the bad ones. They do not want to be a friend with you for their own personal gain. Or because they think they could benefit from having you as a so called friend.

A fake friend does not care if you live or die. They will lie to your face, but behind your back will put you down to others. A fake friend will run at the first sign of any trouble. They will turn against you if there is any sign that they did something wrong. They will take advantage of you whenever they think that they can get away with it. They will try to sway you into believing anything they say is right.

What kind of friend are you?

Wynd Princess

We Are Together

Has there ever been a time in your life when you feel that tough times are yet to come? When you wonder who will be there with you, sometimes that is how I really feel.

There's a man in my life that I love ever so much, but I am now wondering in the back of my mind, if he feels like he should have married me.
I know in my heart, mind, and soul that he does love me. Still, is there someone in this life that can give him more than I can? His family does not like the two of us together at all. I feel so ashamed because they tell everyone that I won't let him see them or his grandchildren. George's daughter and I have butted heads before, but we get along just fine, and her kids are my grandkids, and I love it.

There is one grandchild that I love so much. She was grandmas baby girl, then there is my sweet baby boy who is the apple of grandma's eye.
My baby girl now is all grown up and has a baby boy of her own, so my sweet girl has my great grandson! Wow!

Wynds of Passion: The Love Inside

As for my grandson, Grandpa and I even babysit
him from time to time and I just cannot get
enough. We go out for walks, or we go for rides in
my wheelchair. He says 'go, go, go!' and turns my
chair on. He even tells me love you!

Maybe his sons do not like me because I am
disabled! I know his brother thinks I am no good
for him. That I am just using him for his money
Yeah, right!

I know everyone in the family thinks I am
dragging George down.
Now I can see why his family thinks I am no good
for George. I guess I am not a real lady in their
eyes because I am in a chair.

The thing the kids have to realize is that George is
the FATHER, and if he loves me then there is not a
thing they can do about it. The kids want me to just
leave him alone. So does his niece, and his sisters.
They want George to go back to his ex-wife, their
mother. Wrong answer!

George and I will be together for the rest of our
lives.

What Depression Means to Me

Do you know what depression really is?
There are different kinds of depression, like manic depression. Once in that state it is hard to get out. It's a very deep depression that one really cannot help.

Depression can cause physical problems as well. Not only feelings of worthlessness. Depression can make you feel like you aren't really from the world. It seems like all you want to do is sleep, sleep, sleep. When you feel depressed, you just feel like you are not yourself at all.

That is what depression means to me. What does depression mean to you?

Wynd Princess

Unicorns, Rainbows, and Dreams

The sun is just beginning to rise. The light is starting to trickle down upon the leaves. The morning birds are singing their songs of love. The squirrels are chasing each other through the green grass stopping every now and then to eat the bread, or peanuts that people put out for them. There are deer romping all around, even the bunnies are scampering in their holes that they have dug to hide from the people or to nest in. Even the sweet grass is dancing in the breeze.

Off in the distance, I could see blue waters flowing over a cliff of green into a small sky blue pool below. Beside the pool of blue, was a large oak tree, and I laid down in the soft green grass that was shaded by all the different colors of leaves. The birds gathered along the branches, and began to sing me to sleep.

Hours later as I began to wake up from my sleep, the man of my dreams was laying right next to me. He was watching me sleep. The deer were frolicking all around me, and the bunnies were at my feet tickling them with their noses, and their cotton tails. The man that lay next to me there, asked me to stay with him forever in this land of my dreams. Together, we will never be in any pain ever again. If you are wrong, there is no one to yell at you, and you will never hear the word no.

Just think, we can make love whenever we want under the moon and stars. Here, it never rains, and there are always rainbows for as far as the eye can see. Then we could find our own unicorn and ride those rainbows forever and ever.

Wynd Princess

Note from the Author

Hello, I'm Wynd Princess.

I started just writing for fun, and some family, and friends saw them and said that I should publish them. So, I thought I would try.

I was born in California, Los Angles, in 1963. So, I am fifty-five years of age. I love writing, especially when I am depressed, or have an anxiety attach, because it seems to calm me down faster than any drug on the market can do.

I really hope you like my writings, they are even of my dreams, hopes and fantasies. They might be a bit unorthodox, but this is one of my styles.

Wynd Princess